RETRO
GAME DEV

C64 EDITION

DEREK MORRIS

To all the dreamers in life... It is possible.

TABLE OF CONTENTS

Introduction

Welcome to Retro Game Dev C64 Edition.

Retro game systems from the 1980's hold a special place in my heart. Those early primitive games provided many hours of fun and amazement for a young child. A seed was planted in me that ultimately led to a long career in game development.

The Commodore 64 is the largest selling home computer of all time with 17 million units sold worldwide, and decades later still boasts a thriving development community.

Why Develop for Retro Systems?

Retro games can be created on modern systems like a P.C. or a phone but usually a game engine is utilized that hides the complexities of the underlying hardware. It's these very complexities that teach how to get the most out of the hardware while maximizing efficiency. Such valuable skills are highly sought after in the game industry.

With the recent resurgence of retro games and the revamping of retro systems such as the NES Classic, SNES Classic, and C64 Mini, now's a great time to learn the inner workings of these systems and get your own games out there. Also, the availability of specialized retro game publishers means there's the possibility of having your creation released as a physical boxed product. How cool is that?

About This Book

This book is for those with a desire to create games for the Commodore 64. Whether you're a curious newcomer or are here for nostalgic reasons, I hope it provides a creative springboard that leads to more games for us all to enjoy.

We're privileged in this age of the internet that there's so much development information readily available, but it can be difficult to decipher, thus the aim of this book is to provide a concise guide to developing two mini-games: a space shooter and a platformer, but leave some more advanced features as a further learning exercise for the reader.

Although the BASIC programming language is built into the Commodore 64, it's operation is too slow for all but the most rudimentary of games, therefore we'll use assembly language. Assembly language is well documented elsewhere so this book will cover the basics but focus on the structure of the mini-games and leave the reader to learn more about the assembly language code using suggested literature along with a full code base available to download.

The development tools are P.C. only. The mini-games run on an emulator (various platforms) or a real Commodore 64/128.

Suggested Learning Process

To get the most from this book I suggest the following steps:

- Download the assets from www.retrogamedev.com.
- Run some of the pre-built prg's (Commodore program files) in an emulator or on a real Commodore 64/128.
- Follow through the book trying the experiments and heeding the warnings.

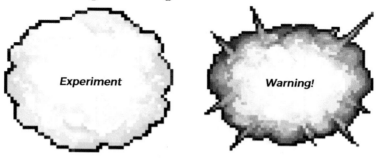

Experiment   Warning!

- Study the supplied code base.

Have fun!

PART I: THE NECESSARY EVIL

Chapter 1: Numbers

The circuits contained within computers are designed to have two states: off and on (or low and high). These states are represented with different electronic voltage levels (usually 0V and 3.3V or 5V). Therefore all information flowing through a computer is a stream of ones and zeros that we call 'machine code' which is unwieldy and error prone for humans.

To alleviate this problem we represent numbers in differing ways for humans to understand and convert to machine code as a final stage.

Bases

As humans we're familiar with the base ten (decimal) number system. It's called base ten because there are ten individual numbers (or digits): 0 through 9. To count past 9 we reuse those same digits i.e. 10, 11, 12 etc. The reasons we use decimal are historic and most likely relate to us having ten fingers (including thumbs) to count with.

If we look past the familiar at exactly how the decimal number system works, we see that each individual digit takes on a specific value with the digits to the right being the lowest amount, increasing in value as we move to the left. These value amounts are the base number value (i.e. 10 for decimal) raised to a power, starting at power 0 for the rightmost digit and increasing as we move left.

Base & Power	10^3	10^2	10^1	10^0
Decimal Value	1000	100	10	1
Example	1	1	0	7

Using the example decimal number 1107, we see there is $1 \times 1000 + 1 \times 100 + 0 \times 10 + 7 \times 1 = 1107$ decimal.

Knowing this information we can look at other number bases as they work the same way.

In base two (or binary) there are two individual digits: 0 and 1. To count past 1 we reuse those same digits i.e. 10, 11, 100, etc.

Base & Power	2^3	2^2	2^1	2^0
Decimal Value	8	4	2	1
Example	1	0	1	1

Using the example binary number 1011, we see there is 1x8 + 0x4 + 1x2 + 1x1 = 11 decimal.

In base sixteen (or hexadecimal) there are sixteen individual digits: 0 through 9 and as we have no more digits to use, the letters A through F. To count past 9 we move to the letter A, then B etc. until F, then 10, 11, 12 etc.

Base & Power	16^3	16^2	16^1	16^0
Decimal Value	4096	256	16	1
Example	1	0	A	C

Using the example hexadecimal number 10AC, we see there is 1x4096 + 0x256 + A(10 in decimal)x16 + C(12 in decimal) x1 = 4268 decimal.

Most calculators have a programmer mode that can convert between number bases. Also note that the upcoming CBM Prg Studio software used throughout this book displays various number base conversions as you hover the mouse cursor over a value.

Bits and Bytes

Returning to the stream of ones and zeros that the computer understands, each individual digit is referred to as a bit (binary digit) i.e. it can have one of two states: a one or a zero as with binary.

To represent a number greater than one, multiple bits are grouped together to form a larger binary number. The industry standard is to group 8 bits together which is called a byte. As 8 is a power of 2 number, it's easy to manipulate and represent by common number bases. The maximum number that can be stored in a byte is 255 if every bit is set to 1, i.e.

Base & Power	2^7	2^6	2^5	2^4	2^3	2^2	2^1	2^0
Decimal Value	128	64	32	16	8	4	2	1
Example	1	1	1	1	1	1	1	1

1x128 + 1x64 + 1x32 + 1x16 + 1x8 + 1x4 + 1x2 + 1x1

= 255 decimal.

If we need to use a higher value, then multiple bytes are used together. Two bytes used together is called a word and can store a maximum value of 65535.

16 bit, 2 Byte Number (Word)	
High Byte (MSB)	Low Byte (LSB)

High Byte (MSB)							
Base & Power	2^{15}	2^{14}	2^{13}	2^{12}	2^{11}	2^{10}	2^9	2^8

Low Byte (LSB)							
Base & Power	2^7	2^6	2^5	2^4	2^3	2^2	2^1	2^0

The lower value byte is called the low byte or least significant byte (LSB) and when this maxes out at 255 the high byte or most significant byte (MSB) comes into use.

Negative numbers can be represented by using the highest value bit in a byte as a negative flag. If using this mechanism, the number is known as signed and can store values in the range of -128 to +127. Otherwise it's unsigned and can store values in the range of 0 to 255.

Uses

A common way of specifying the base of a number is with an appropriate symbol. i.e.

%11111111 = binary
$FF = hexadecimal
255 = decimal (no symbol)

A binary representation may be used if you use each bit as a flag and set or read bits individually. A hexadecimal representation may be used when referring to a memory location or a list byte of values in a compact form. E.g.

$FA	$AB	$11	$D6	$1E	$C2	$5B	$28	$70	$9F

Each digit represents 4 bits (called a nibble), so 2 digits represent a full 8-bit byte.

The decision is left to the programmer over which number bases are convenient as all numbers are ultimately converted to binary machine code before they can used by the computer.

Chapter 2: Commodore 64 Hardware

Of the many computer chips that make up the C64, we're primarily concerned with four of them here. The 6510 microprocessor runs the computer program, the VIC-II graphics chip displays images to the screen, the SID sound chip synthesizes a range of audio, and a set of memory chips store bytes of information.

6510

The 6510 microprocessor is a variant of the popular 6502 which was also used in the Atari 2600, Apple II and Nintendo Entertainment System (NES).

It's an 8-bit microprocessor which means that the units of information it operates on are 8 bits (1 byte) in size.

The 6510 has a set of 56 instructions (8-bit opcodes) that tell it which operation to perform. These instructions and the data they operate on are placed into memory for the microprocessor to read and process. All of the instructions and data combined make up the program to be run.

When an instruction is run, the data being processed is copied into one of the special areas of memory built into the microprocessor called a register. The 6510 registers of concern to us when creating our games are:

- A – The accumulator. Handles arithmetic and logic.
- X and Y – General purpose and indexing.
- P – Processor status flags. Results of operations.
- PC – Program counter. Next instruction to be run.

Essentially the 6510 reads an instruction and any required data from the memory location stored in the PC, processes the data, writes the result back to memory (if required), and increments the PC, ready to repeat over and over until the program ends.

VIC-II

The VIC-II graphics chip transfers an area of memory onto the screen that's interpreted depending on the screen mode. In bitmap mode each pixel is set individually for a resolution of 320x200 pixels. However, this is generally too restrictive in terms of memory usage and speed, so we'll use character mode which is 40 columns x 25 rows of characters. These characters can be multicolor (4 color, 4 double width x 8 pixels) or hires (2 color, 8x8 pixels).

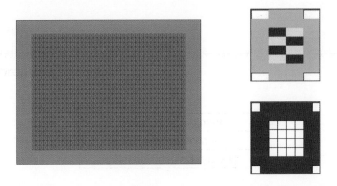

There are 8 hardware sprites available that can be drawn anywhere on the screen. These are also available in multicolor (4 color, 12 double width x 21 pixels) or hires (2 color, 24x21 pixels).

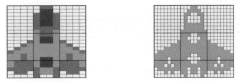

The VIC-II is controlled by setting the values in screen memory and color memory, and setting the values of specific memory locations that are mapped to the chip itself. These are called memory mapped registers.

SID

The SID chip can play 3 voices simultaneously. Each of the 3 voices is capable of producing 4 types of waveform – triangle, sawtooth, pulse, and noise.

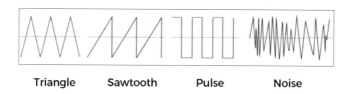

Triangle   Sawtooth   Pulse   Noise

You can further control the sound by setting the frequency of each note played and the Attack Decay Sustain Release (ADSR) envelope. Attack is the speed at which the note reaches full volume. Decay is the rate the volume falls to mid-range. Sustain is the mid-range volume level which is held for a while, and Release is the rate the volume drops off to zero.

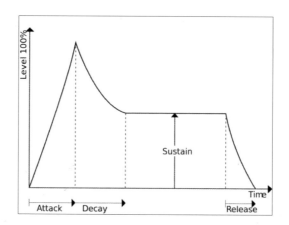

Many different sounds can be generated by altering the wave type, frequency and ADSR envelope of the notes being played. These values can also be changed dynamically as the note is being played for interesting effects. The SID is also controlled with memory mapped registers.

Memory

The 6510 uses a 16-bit program counter (PC) to address memory locations, therefore it can see 65536 individual bytes of memory (or 64K). These memory locations are arranged into sections of usage type shown here with a memory map.

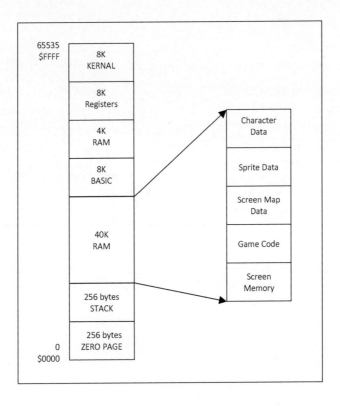

The C64 has the ability to switch out the BASIC and KERNAL if they're not required, to free up more space for user programs. However, as our mini-games don't need the extra space, the default configuration is used.

The VIC-II can only access 16K at one time so there are certain limitations to where you can place screen and graphics data (See C64 Programmer's Reference Guide for more details).

Chapter 3: 6502 Assembly Language

Assembly language is used as a convenient way for humans to work with the opcodes required for a microprocessor to function. Rather than having to use pure binary numbers, three character mnemonics represent each opcode, and a number base of programmer choice is used for the data (usually hexadecimal).

A program called an assembler converts the assembly program into binary machine code for the target microprocessor to run.

The advantage of working with assembly language over a high level language such as C/C++ is that each mnemonic maps directly to a single microprocessor opcode, so the programmer has complete control. The downside being that it can take much longer to code the required functionality.

BASIC on the other hand is an interpreted language which means that each command is translated to microprocessor form as the program is running. This has the result of executing much slower than a prebuilt program.

As there are many excellent resources available on assembly language programming, we'll cover a subset here and leave it as a reader exercise to gain more knowledge from one of the resources listed in <u>Chapter 21</u>.

Instructions

Two of the most commonly used assembly mnemonics are:

- lda – Load the Accumulator
- sta – Store the Accumulator

These instructions transfer a single byte of data between the Accumulator (A register) and one of the 65536 available memory locations. They are analogous to the Commodore BASIC PEEK and POKE commands.

When specifying numbers in assembly (for the assembler used in this book), the prefixes $ for hexadecimal, and % for binary are used. No prefix indicates decimal.

The # symbol is used to specify a numeric value. If there is no # symbol then we're referring to a memory location (address).

Anything following a ; symbol is a comment and is ignored by the assembler. This symbol can be inserted before a line of code to disable it (known as commenting out the code).

An example of these in a program is:

```
lda #2          ; decimal 2 (value) -> A
sta $0400       ; A -> hex 400 (address)
```

The first line loads the number 2 into the Accumulator (A register). The second line stores the value in the Accumulator (2) into the memory location specified by the address ($0400).

This happens to put a letter B onto to screen at the top left character position (More on that later).

Now let's copy a value stored in one memory location into another memory location.

```
lda $0400       ; 400 hex (address) -> A
sta $0401       ; A -> 401 hex (address)
```

Note that you can't copy a byte of memory directly from one memory location to another. You must go through one of the microprocessor registers.

Addressing

The addressing mode refers to which exact opcode is used based on the data that's supplied with the mnemonic.

An example of different addressing modes using lda is:

```
lda #2        ; immediate mode
lda $2        ; zero page mode
lda $2000     ; absolute mode
```

Remember that the $ symbol is not connected to the addressing mode. It specifies a hexadecimal number. These could be decimal or binary. The convention is to use hexadecimal numbers when specifying memory addresses.

Immediate mode takes a number value and uses 2 bytes, 1 for the 8-bit opcode and 1 for the 8-bit value. It takes 2 clock cycles (a measurement of microprocessor speed) to execute.

Zero Page mode takes an address in the range 0->255 and uses 2 bytes, 1 for the 8-bit opcode and 1 for the 8-bit address. It takes 3 clock cycles to execute.

Absolute mode takes an address in the range 256->65535 and uses 3 bytes, 1 for the 8-bit opcode, 1 for the address high byte, and 1 for the address low byte. It takes 4 clock cycles to execute.

We can see that Zero Page addressing (memory locations 0->255) is more efficient than absolute addressing as only 1 byte is needed to specify the address. It's recommended to make use of Zero Page memory locations as much as possible. The C64 BASIC and KERNAL do make use of many Zero Page locations but as our mini-games don't use those, Zero Page is free to utilize.

Indexing

Some additional addressing modes are the indexed modes that are used to look up data from a list using an indexed offset.

```
myList   byte 15,  6,  17,  1,  18,  2,  4,  14,  12,  5

         ldx #2
         lda myList,x ; 3rd item in the list (zero based) -> A
```

Here the ldx instruction loads the number 2 into the X register. Then the value in the X register (2), is used to look up into the list and copy the third item (17) into the Accumulator.

There are more advanced indexed addressing modes available but they all operate on the same mechanism of using values to look up into a list of other values.

Flow Control

Most instructions write a result to the P register.

N	V		B	D	I	Z	C

An example is where the lda instruction will write a 0 to the Z bit of the P register if a 0 was loaded and a 1 otherwise.

These bits are then tested against to perform program flow control. For example, a beq instruction will redirect the program to a memory location specified if the Z flag equals zero.

Other ways to redirect program flow is to use a jmp instruction to jump to the supplied memory location and continue executing, or a jsr(jump to subroutine)/rts(return from subroutine) pair to redirect program flow to a subroutine and return to the original memory location when finished.

PART II: STARTING TO PROGRAM

Chapter 4: I.D.E.

In order to create our games we need a way to convert the assembly language we write into machine code that the Commodore 64 can understand, and to package it together with our data into a program file that can be run.

The software used to convert assembly language into machine code is called an assembler. Back in the 1980's the assembler was usually used on the Commodore 64 itself. It was a laborious process to type all the instructions and assemble into machine code. There were few editing tools available and the hardware itself was slow with minimal resources.

An I.D.E. (Integrated Development Environment) is a suite of related tools combined into a single program to run on a host computer (in our case a Microsoft Windows™ P.C.). These tools can include an assembler (sometimes called a cross-assembler as it assembles code for a different machine), code editor, debugger, sprite and screen editors, and audio editor. The resulting program can then be run on the same PC in an emulator or on the Commodore 64 hardware.

For this book we use an I.D.E. called CBM Prg Studio due to its extensive feature set, ease of use, and support for all of the Commodore machines. But most importantly the incredible ongoing support from its creator, Arthur Jordison.

CBM Prg Studio can be downloaded for free from http://www.ajordison.co.uk/download.html. Please make a donation if you find this software useful in order that it can continue to be supported in the future.

In this chapter we'll create a simple assembly program to demonstrate the usage of the assembler and debugger tools available in the I.D.E.

There are often multiple ways to select the same option. i.e. toolbar menus, toolbar icons, and function keys. For convention the toolbar menus are stated throughout the book.

Setup

Install and run CBM Prg Studio on your Microsoft Windows™
P.C. and you're presented with the main I.D.E. screen.

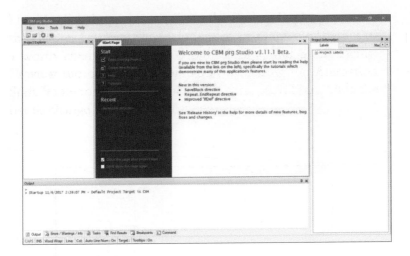

- Select **Tools->Options->Project** and set the **Default
  Location**. This is where future created projects will be
  saved to.

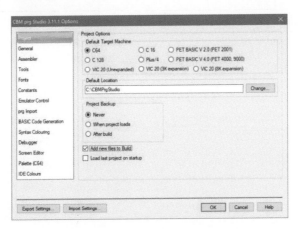

- Select **Assembler** at the left of the same dialog box and set **Var/label dump** and **Assembly Dump** to **None**, check **Optimise Absolute modes to Zero page**, and uncheck **Report page boundary crossings**. These options remove the unnecessary build output and warnings for our work.

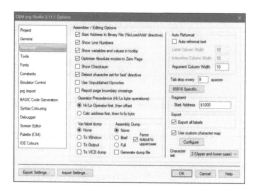

- Select **OK** to accept the settings.

- Select **File->New Project** to create a new project.
- Select **Next** to accept **C 64** as the target machine.

- Enter the Project Name. e.g. chapter4.
- Select **Next** to proceed.

- Select **Create** to create the new project.

The new project contains some pre-created directories in the Project Explorer to the left.

- Right click on **Assembly Files** in the Project Explorer.
- Select **Add New File**.
- Name the file. e.g. **main.asm**.
- Select **OK** to create and add the new assembly file.

You're now presented with a blank assembly file ready to accept assembly language instructions.

Note that the assembly code used throughout this book is written for use with CBM Prg Studio, but could work just as well with an alternate assembler (both cross development and C64 native). However, the code may need some tweaks to build correctly. E.g. the macro syntax, the byte directives etc. Refer to the particular assembler documentation for more details.

First Program

Let's write our first assembly language program.

Memory locations and labels are entered in the left most column. Assembly instructions are indented by one tab. All text following a semicolon is a comment for clarity and is ignored by the assembler. Enter the program as shown.

main.asm

```
*=$0801
        lda #4        ; decimal 4 (value) -> A
        ldx #5        ; decimal 5 (value) -> X
        ldy #6        ; decimal 6 (value) -> Y
```

The program begins by defining the memory location where the assembler should start placing the assembled code. $0801 is the default memory location for Commodore 64 BASIC programs to begin executing (More on this later).

Then there are three instructions which load the accumulator, the x register, and the y register, with some test values.

Debugger

In order to test this program we'll use the built-in debugger tool.

- Select **File->Save Project** to save your work.
- Select **Debugger->Debug Program** to assemble the program to machine code and open the debugger tool.

If there are errors when assembling the code, the error messages will display in the Output window. The usual culprits are typos or incorrect tabs.

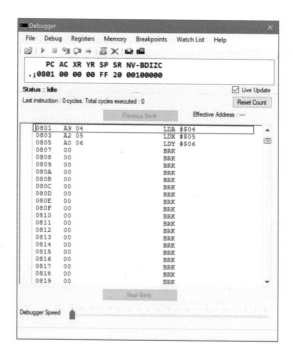

When the program assembles correctly, various debugger windows will open. We're only concerned with the main Debugger window for now.

The Debugger shows the register values in the top window and the memory location (left), assembled machine code (middle) and assembly instructions (right) in the main window. The **PC** (Program Counter) register has the value $0801 which is the start location of our code in memory, and this will be the first instruction to be run. The **AC** (Accumulator), **XR** (X Register) and **YR** (Y Register) values all start at zero.

- Select **Debug->Step Program** to execute the first instruction.

The **PC** register changes to $0803 which is our start point plus the size of the first instruction (2 bytes). Also the **AC** register changes to 04 which is the value we set.

- Select **Debug->Step Program** twice more to execute the second and third instructions.

The **PC** register changes to $0805 and the **XR** register changes to 05. Then the **PC** register changes to $0807 and the **YR** register changes to 06.

This concludes our program and any subsequent **Step Program**'s will interpret the 00 in memory as a break (BRK) instruction and reset the program counter to the start of memory.

In order to re-run the program, you can either close the debugger window and start the debug process again or

- Select **Registers->Clear** to reset the register values.
- Select **Registers->Set** and set the **Program Counter** value to $0801 which is the memory location of the start of our program.

You've now successfully built and debugged your first Commodore 64 assembly program.

Further I.D.E. functionality is explained in the tutorials which can be accessed from the **Help->Contents** menu in the **Introduction->Tutorials** section.

Although the information available in the debugger is extensive, a much quicker way of debugging problems is to print the contents of a variable to the screen. The LIBSCREEN_DEBUG macros are available in the library code (see Chapter 6 for information on macros). Note that these use kernal code and are slow to execute.

Chapter 5: Emulator

The Versatile Commodore Emulator (VICE) can be downloaded for free from http://vice-emu.sourceforge.net/.

Setup

Install VICE and run x64.exe (Details are for a Microsoft Windows™ P.C. Other platforms are very similar).

You're presented with the Commodore 64 home screen.

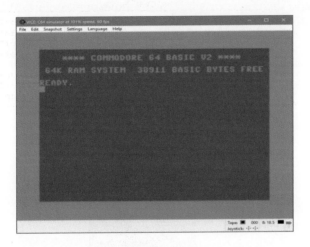

- Select **Settings->Save settings on exit.**
- Select **Settings->Refresh rate->1/1.** This stabilizes the frame rate.
- Select **Settings->Sound settings->Sound playback.**
- Select **Settings->C64 model settings->C64 NTSC.** This selects the TV standard. NTSC is recommended as it runs at 60 frames per second but PAL also works with the mini-games in this book.
- Select **Settings->Video settings->VICII Renderer->Render filter->CRT emulation.** For those of us who love CRT TV's.

- Select **Settings->Joystick settings->Joystick settings**. Configure the input method for up/down/left/right/fire.

Note: Check **Settings->Warp mode** is disabled if the emulator ever runs very fast.

Running a prg File

To load and run prg file directly in the emulator, drag the prg file onto the emulator window (Prebuilt prg's are included with the book assets download).

To build and run a prg file from within CBM Prg Studio, first setup the emulator location.

- Select **Tools->Options->Emulator Control** and set the **Emulator and Path** to point to the installed location of the VICE emulator.

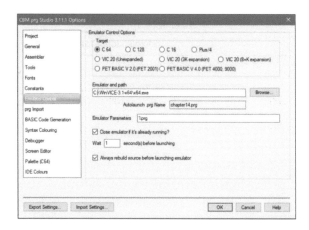

- Select **Build->Project->And Run** to assemble all of the source files in a project to a prg file, then run the prg file in the VICE emulator.

Chapter 6: Code Framework

Open chapter6.cbmprj in CBM Prg Studio.

Organization

The code for this book uses a number of naming conventions to keep everything neat and tidy. E.g. prefixing library files with 'lib' or game files with 'game'. Here's the full list:

Type	Example
Library files	libScreen.asm
Game files	gameMain.asm
Constant Values	Black
Variable Values	playerActive
Registers / Memory Locations	BGCOL0
Macros	LIBSCREEN_WAIT_V
Subroutines	libScreenWait
Global Labels	gMLoop
Local(Macro) Labels	@loop

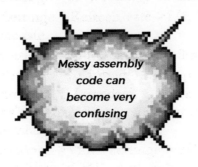

Messy assembly code can become very confusing

Memory Layout

The file gameMemory.asm maps out the location of game code, game assets (sprites, maps, characters), and the hardware registers showing how they fit into the C64 memory map (See Chapter 2 – Memory).

Keeping all memory references in this one file helps to organize memory. The assembler will place code after any *= directives and any further code will be placed after that.

Build order is setup in **Project->Properties**. By keeping gameMain.asm at the top and gameMemory.asm at the bottom, all of our game code will follow the $0801 memory location and any game assets can be placed into gameMemory.asm.

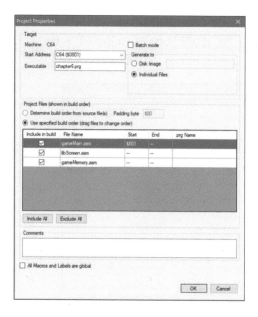

Macros vs Subroutines

A macro is a section of code that's surrounded by the defm/endm keywords. For example:

```
                          libScreen.asm
; Waits for a given scanline
defm    LIBSCREEN_WAIT_V    ; /1 = Scanline (Value)

@loop   lda #/1             ; Scanline -> A
        cmp RASTER          ; Compare A to current raster line
        bne @loop           ; Loop if raster line not reached 255

        endm
```

The macro can take parameters (like a function or method in a high level language) and the code is copied in place to everywhere it's called, thus uses more code memory the more times it's used. Macros can call subroutines but can't call other macros. The suffix used in this book describes the type and number of parameters. E.g. _VAA is 1 value and 2 address parameters.

By contrast, a subroutine takes the form of:

```
; Waits for scanline 255
libScreenWait

lSWLoop lda #255           ; Scanline -> A
        cmp Raster         ; Compare A to current raster line
        bne lSWLoop        ; Loop if raster line not reached 255

        rts

        ; Called like this
        jsr libScreenWait
```

The subroutine cannot take parameters and the jsr instruction runs the code and returns after using only one set of code however many times it's called. However, the jsr and rts instructions themselves take some time to execute so it's slower to run than the macro version. Subroutines can call other subroutines and macros (technically macros are not called as a copy of the macro code is placed at the call position).

Choosing between using macros vs subroutines is a tradeoff between code size and execution speed.

BASIC Autoloader

When a program is loaded into the C64, the default behavior is to run a BASIC program at memory location $0801. The following short 15 byte BASIC program runs our assembly code program by executing a '10 SYS 2064' BASIC command which runs the code at $0810 (15 bytes after $0801). This short BASIC program can be auto created by CBM Prg Studio with **Tools->Generate SYS() Call**.

gameMain.asm
```
*=$0801 ; 10 SYS (2064)

        byte $0E, $08, $0A, $00, $9E, $20, $28, $32
        byte $30, $36, $34, $29, $00, $00, $00

        ; Our code starts at $0810 (2064 decimal)
        ; after the 15 bytes for the BASIC loader
```

Character Sets

The C64 has two character sets each containing 256 individual 8x8 pixel characters. One of these character sets is active at any one time. They can be switched at the C64 BASIC screen with Shift & Commodore Key on C64 hardware, or Shift & Control in the emulator, and the text will change between upper and lower case. We override these characters with our own custom character sets in later chapters.

Select **Tools->Character Editor** to open the character editor.

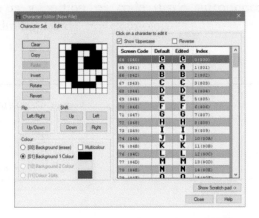

Notice the **Show Uppercase** and **Reverse** checkboxes. **Show Uppercase** switches between the first and second character sets. The index column changes from 0->127 and 256->383. The **Reverse** checkbox switches between the upper and lower half of the selected character set, so with **Reverse** checked you get 128->255 and 384->511.

The thing to watch out for here is that when using an ascii character to index into the Commodore character set you may not always get the expected results.

The default behavior for CBM Prg Studio is to map lower case characters in single quotes to the first character set so 'a' = Index 1 = A displayed on screen, whereas 'A' = Index 65 = ♠ displayed on screen.

Each of the characters can be accessed directly using the index number without quotes. E.g. Filling screen memory with the number 2 would produce all 'B' characters on screen.

Further info on the various configurable character mapping setups can be found from the **Help->Contents** menu in the **Using The Assembler->Directives** and **Using The Assembler->Data Types** sections.

Game Initialize

To begin we set the screen colors and fill the screen and color memory in gameMain.asm.

gameMain.asm

```
; Set border and background colors
; The last 3 parameters are not used yet
LIBSCREEN_SETCOLORS Blue, White, Black, Black, Black

; Fill 1000 bytes (40x25) of screen memory
LIBSCREEN_SET1000 SCREENRAM, 'a'

; Fill 1000 bytes (40x25) of color memory
LIBSCREEN_SET1000 COLORRAM, Black
```

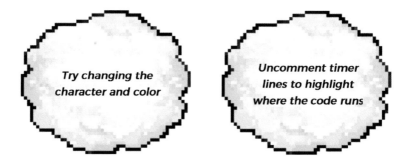

Try changing the character and color

Uncomment timer lines to highlight where the code runs

Game Loop

Every frame we wait for scanline 255, then run the game code before looping back around. The code is run outside of the visible display area so that we don't update display registers while drawing and cause screen tearing.

gameMain.asm

```
gMLoop
        LIBSCREEN_WAIT_V 255
        ;inc EXTCOL ; start code timer change border color
        ; Game update code goes here
        ;dec EXTCOL ; end code timer reset border color
        jmp gMLoop
```

Chapter 6 Result

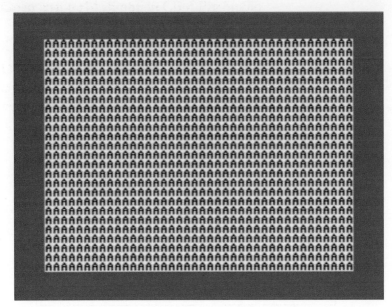

PART III: LET'S MAKE A SPACE SHOOTER

Chapter 7: Create a Stellar Spaceship

Open chapter7.cbmprj in CBM Prg Studio.

Player Sprite

Double click the sprites.spt file in the Project Explorer to open the chapter 7 sprite file. Included are two sample spaceship sprites.

The first is a hires version.

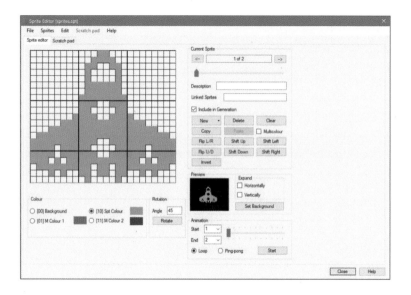

Click the Current Sprite right arrow to see a multicolor version. Notice the Multicolour checkbox and the use of the extra two colors.

[10] Spt Colour is the sprites unique color. [01] M Colour 1 and [11] M Colour 2 are shared between all sprites. These values are set in the sprite editor for preview purposes only and are not exported along with the sprite data. The in-game values are set in game code later.

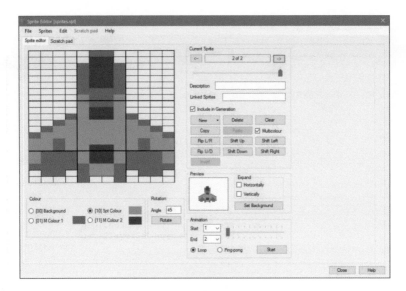

Try creating your
own spaceship
sprites

Save the sprite file with **File->Save**, then export a binary
version of the sprites to be used in game with **File->Export-
>To Binary File**. Choose to save all the sprites and name the
file sprites.bin in the project directory (Overwrite if necessary).

The exported sprite data is added to the program by including it in the memory map. The *= $3000 directive tells the assembler to start placing data at memory location $3000 onwards (See C64 Programmer's Reference Guide for more details on alternative locations to place sprite data).

gameMemory.asm

```
; 192 decimal * 64(sprite size) = 12288(hex $3000)
SPRITERAM       = 192
* = $3000
        incbin sprites.bin
```

In the game initialize code, the sprite multicolors are set (these are the global colors for all sprites) and a subroutine is called to initialize the player.

gameMain.asm

```
; Set sprite multicolors
LIBSPRITE_SETMULTICOLORS_VV MediumGray, DarkGray

; Initialize the player
jsr gamePlayerInit
```

The player is initialized by enabling the sprite, setting the current animation frame, and setting the sprite colors.

gameplayer.asm

```
gamePlayerInit

        LIBSPRITE_ENABLE_AV              playerSprite, True
        LIBSPRITE_SETFRAME_AV            playerSprite, PlayerFrame
        LIBSPRITE_SETCOLOR_AV            playerSprite, LightGray
        LIBSPRITE_MULTICOLORENABLE_AV    playerSprite, True

        rts
```

Try changing PlayerFrame to your created sprite number

Also toggle the sprite multicolor with True or False

Sprite color information is set in code, not exported

Player Movement

Player movement is performed by updating the latest input information from the joystick and updating the player code.

gameMain.asm

```
; Update the library
jsr libInputUpdate

; Update the game
jsr gamePlayerUpdate
```

The player update code then calls a subroutine to update the player position. This is an additional subroutine call to keep the code neat and allow for more subroutines to be called from here in later chapters.

gamePlayer.asm

```
gamePlayerUpdate

        jsr gamePlayerUpdatePosition

        rts
```

The player position is updated by taking the joystick input and adding or subtracting the constant player speed in the vertical or horizontal direction.

The player position is then clamped to a screen rectangle (so that the spaceship doesn't fly off the screen), and finally the player sprite position is updated with the new player position.

gamePlayer.asm

```
gamePlayerUpdatePosition

        LIBINPUT_GETHELD GameportLeftMask
        bne gPUPRight
        LIBMATH_SUB16BIT_AAVVAA playerXHigh, PlayerXLow, 0,
PlayerHorizontalSpeed, playerXHigh, PlayerXLow
gPUPRight
        LIBINPUT_GETHELD GameportRightMask
        bne gPUPUp
        LIBMATH_ADD16BIT_AAVVAA playerXHigh, PlayerXLow, 0,
PlayerHorizontalSpeed, playerXHigh, PlayerXLow
gPUPUp
        LIBINPUT_GETHELD GameportUpMask
        bne gPUPDown
        LIBMATH_SUB8BIT_AVA PlayerY, PlayerVerticalSpeed,
PlayerY
gPUPDown
        LIBINPUT_GETHELD GameportDownMask
        bne gPUPEndmove
        LIBMATH_ADD8BIT_AVA PlayerY, PlayerVerticalSpeed,
PlayerY
gPUPEndmove

        ; clamp the player x position
        LIBMATH_MIN16BIT_AAVV playerXHigh, playerXLow,
PlayerXMaxHigh, PlayerXMaxLow
        LIBMATH_MAX16BIT_AAVV playerXHigh, playerXLow,
PlayerXMinHigh, PlayerXMinLow

        ; clamp the player y position
        LIBMATH_MIN8BIT_AV playerY, PlayerYMax
        LIBMATH_MAX8BIT_AV playerY, PlayerYMin

        ; set the sprite position
        LIBSPRITE_SETPOSITION_AAAA playerSprite, playerXHigh,
PlayerXLow, PlayerY

        rts
```

**Try changing the
Player X & Y
Min/Max constants**

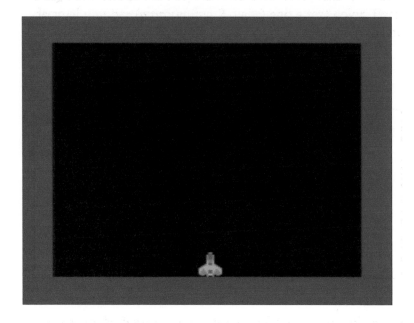

Chapter 8: Shoot the Bullets

Open chapter8.cbmprj in CBM Prg Studio.

Software Sprites

The C64 can display 8 hardware sprites at a time (excluding advanced multiplexing techniques – see Chapter 20). Therefore, in order to display many bullets we use a software sprite drawing technique. This uses the 40x25 characters on the screen as substitute sprites.

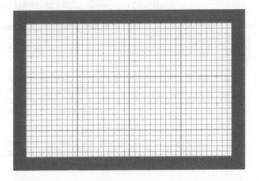

A drawback with this technique is that when animating these software sprites they can only be moved a full character size at a time i.e. 8 pixels horizontally or vertically.

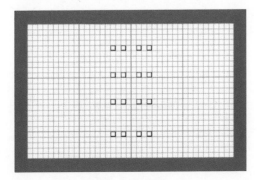

To get around this limitation we draw multiple offset animation frames and cycle through them before moving to the next character position.

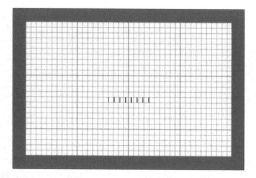

In this implementation there are only separate animation frames for the horizontal direction. As the bullets move so quickly vertically, it's fine to move a character at a time in that direction.

An extra macro call is added to the gamePlayerUpdatePosition subroutine to calculate the player screen character position and offset. This is calculated by dividing the position by 8, as there are 8 pixels in each character. Offsets are also added to allow adjustment of the bullet firing location from the origin (top-left) of the player sprite.

gamePlayer.asm

```
    ; update the player char positions
    LIBSCREEN_PIXELTOCHAR_AAVAVAAAA playerXHigh, playerXLow, 12,
playerY, 40, playerXChar, playerXOffset, playerYChar,
playerYOffset
```

Try changing the x & y positional offsets

The player code now calls a subroutine to fire the bullets.

gamePlayer.asm

```
gamePlayerUpdate

        . . .
        jsr gamePlayerUpdateFiring

        rts
```

This bullet firing code checks the joystick fire button and if pressed creates a new bullet at the previously calculated character and offset positions.

gamePlayer.asm

```
gamePlayerUpdateFiring

        ; do fire after the ship has been clamped to position
        ; so that the bullet lines up
        LIBINPUT_GETFIREPRESSED
        bne gPUFNofire

        GAMEBULLETS_FIRE_AAAVV playerXChar, playerXOffset,
playerYChar, White, True
gPUFNofire

        rts
```

The bullet movement is performed by a subroutine call. This update code loops through each active bullet and moves it upwards toward the top of the screen (A single row at the top of the screen is left blank to add the score text in a future chapter).

gameMain.asm

```
        jsr gameBulletsUpdate
```

Custom Characters

We create the frames of animation for the bullets by customizing the C64 character set. This is achieved by using the character editor.

Double click the characters.cst file in the Project Explorer to open the chapter 8 character file. The character numbers 64->71 have been reserved for the bullet animation frames. These have been chosen to keep the letters and numbers before them intact for future usage (although any could be used).

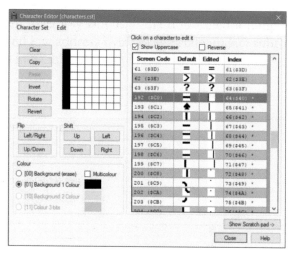

Try creating your own bullet animation frames

As with sprites there's a multicolor option for characters. The space shooter mini-game uses hires characters only (We explore the usage of multicolor characters in Chapter 14).

Save the character file with **Character Set->Save**, then export a binary version of the characters to be used in-game with **Character Set->Export->To Binary File**. Choose to export 80 characters starting at character 0 and name the file characters.bin in the project directory (Overwrite if necessary).

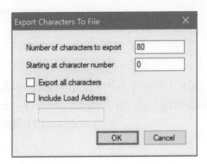

The exported character data is added to the program by including it in the memory map. The *= $3800 directive tells the assembler to start placing data at memory location $3800 onwards (See C64 Programmer's Reference Guide for more details on alternative locations to place character data).

gameMemory.asm

```
* = $3800
        incbin characters.bin
```

Then we tell the C64 to override the default character set by setting the memory location of our custom characters (See C64 Programmer's Reference Guide for character data mappings i.e. where the 14 comes from).

gameMain.asm

```
; Set the memory location of the custom character set
        LIBSCREEN_SETCHARMEMORY 14
```

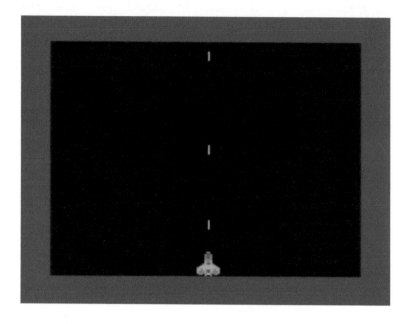

Chapter 9: Start the Alien Invasion

Open chapter9.cbmprj in CBM Prg Studio.

Alien Sprites

Double click the sprites.spt file in the Project Explorer to open the chapter 9 sprite file. Added to the two spaceship sprites are one multicolor alien and one hires alien.

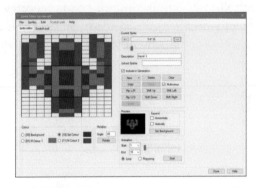

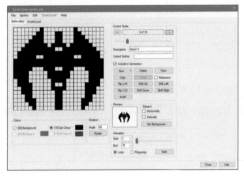

Try creating your own alien sprites

In the game initialize code, a subroutine is called to initialize the aliens.

gameMain.asm

```
jsr gameAliensInit
```

As with the player, the aliens are initialized by enabling the sprite, setting the current animation frame, and setting the sprite colors. However, this time the code loops around for each of the 7 aliens (AliensMax=7).

gameAliens.asm

```
gameAliensInit

        ldx #0
        stx aliensSprite
gAILoop
        inc aliensSprite ; x+1

        jsr gameAliensGetVariables

        LIBSPRITE_ENABLE_AV     aliensSprite, True
        LIBSPRITE_SETFRAME_AA   aliensSprite, aliensFrame
        LIBSPRITE_SETCOLOR_AA   aliensSprite, aliensColor
        LIBSPRITE_MULTICOLORENABLE_AA aliensSprite,
aliensMultiColor

        jsr gameAliensSetVariables

        inx
        cpx #AliensMax
        bne gAILoop ; loop for each alien

        rts
```

Try changing the alien sprite values and constants

AliensMax can't be > 7 as there are only 8 C64 sprites

Also included are twelve frames of an explosion animation. Preview the animation by setting the Animation Start frame to 5, End frame to 16, then press Start. Slide the bar to change the animation speed.

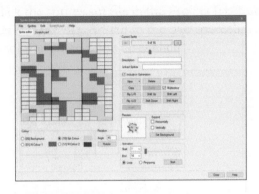

Try creating your own explosion animation

Alien Movement

Alien movement is performed by adding a subroutine call to update the alien code.

gameMain.asm

```
; Update the game
jsr gameAliensUpdate
```

As with the player, the alien code calls a subroutine to update the positions, and another to update the firing.

gameAliens.asm

```
gameAliensUpdate

        . . .
        jsr gameAliensUpdatePosition
        jsr gameAliensUpdateFiring
        . . .

        rts
```

The alien positions are updated by cycling through a table of offset values to the aliens original position.

gameAliens.asm

```
              ; right
aliensXMoveArray byte    0,   0,   1,   1,   1,   2,   2,   3,   4,   5
              byte    6,   7,   8,   9,  10,  11,  12,  13,  14,  15
              byte   16,  17,  18,  19,  20,  21,  22,  23,  24,  25
              byte   26,  27,  28,  29,  30,  31,  32,  33,  34,  35
              byte   36,  37,  38,  39,  39,  40,  40,  40,  41,  41

              ; left
              byte   41,  41,  40,  40,  40,  39,  39,  38,  37,  36
              byte   35,  34,  33,  32,  31,  30,  29,  28,  27,  26
              byte   25,  24,  23,  22,  21,  20,  19,  18,  17,  16
              byte   15,  14,  13,  12,  11,  10,   9,   8,   7,   6
              byte    5,   4,   3,   2,   2,   1,   1,   1,   0,   0
```

Try changing the alien movement offset values

AliensXMoveNumIndices must = number of table values

There's a tool available at **Tools->Data Generator** that can export lists of values based on mathematical functions. These could be plugged into the alien movement table for more advanced movement (Maybe multiple tables for different types of movement).

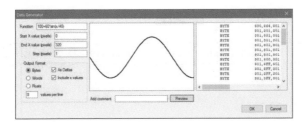

The aliens fire continuously on a frame delay (AliensFireDelay constant). Also note that the last parameter passed to GAME_BULLETSFIRE_AAAVV is False to make the bullets fire down the screen instead of up like the player.

gameAliens.asm

```
gameAliensUpdateFiring

        lda playerActive ; only fire if the player is alive
        beq gAUFDontfire

        ldy aliensFire
        iny
        sty aliensFire
        cpy #AliensFireDelay
        beq gAUFFire
        jmp gAUFDontfire
gAUFFire

        GAMEBULLETS_FIRE_AAAVV aliensXChar, aliensXOffset,
aliensYChar, Yellow, False

        lda #0
        sta aliensFire
gAUFDontfire

        rts
```

Collisions

Now that we have a player, aliens and bullets, collisions are calculated so we can trigger an explosion if the player or aliens are hit by a bullet.

The C64 has hardware registers to indicate a collision between sprites, and between sprites and characters. However, they only indicate that a collision has occurred and give no extra information about which specific background character is involved. As we need to know which bullet is involved in a collision in order to destroy it, we'll implement custom collision detection.

As with the player, each alien position update calls LIBSCREEN_PIXELTOCHAR_AAVAVAAAA to calculate its current character positions.

gameAliens.asm

```
; update the alien char positions
    LIBSCREEN_PIXELTOCHAR_AAVAVAAAA aliensXHigh, aliensXLow,
12, aliensY, 40, aliensXChar, aliensXOffset, aliensYChar,
aliensYOffset
```

Try changing the x and y positional offsets

The player code now calls a subroutine to update the collisions.

gamePlayer.asm

```
gamePlayerUpdate

    . . .
    jsr gamePlayerUpdateCollisions
    . . .

    rts
```

In the gamePlayerUpdateCollisions subroutine, the GAMEBULLETS_COLLIDED macro is called, passing in the player's character positions, which are then checked against the character positions for each active bullet. If they're the same then a collision has been detected. The bullet code will then destroy the bullet and the player code runs the explosion animation.

gamePlayer.asm

```
gamePlayerUpdateCollisions

        GAMEBULLETS_COLLIDED playerXChar, playerYChar, False
        beq gPUCNocollision
        lda #False
        sta playerActive
        ; run explosion animation
        LIBSPRITE_SETCOLOR_AV      playerSprite, Yellow
        LIBSPRITE_PLAYANIM_AVVVV   playerSprite, 4, 15, 3, False

gPUCNocollision

        rts
```

The same thing happens for each alien.

gameAliens.asm

```
jsr gameAliensUpdateCollisions
```

gameAliens.asm

```
gameAliensUpdateCollisions

        GAMEBULLETS_COLLIDED aliensXChar, aliensYChar, True

        beq gAUCNocollision
        ; run explosion animation
        LIBSPRITE_PLAYANIM_AVVVV      aliensSprite, 4, 15, 3,
False

        LIBSPRITE_SETCOLOR_AV          aliensSprite, Yellow
        LIBSPRITE_MULTICOLORENABLE_AV aliensSprite, True

        lda #False
        sta aliensActive
gAUCNocollision

        rts
```

Sprites can move around the screen pixel by pixel and therefore don't always line up with the 8x8 pixel character boundaries. To aid with the efficiency of the collision calculations, these pixel offsets are ignored. This has the effect of the character collision checks shifting around depending on the sprite's position.

Another speed optimization is to calculate a center character location and check the characters immediately adjacent to the left and right. These three characters form a primitive bounding box.

Frame 1   Frame 2

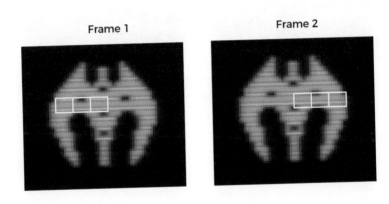

Tradeoffs like this are commonplace in game development as a compromise between performance and visual accuracy. In this case, as the bullets move so fast, the inaccuracy is hardly noticeable.

The LIBSCREEN_PIXELTOCHAR_AAVAVAAAA macro does also calculate the x and y pixel offsets that could be used for pixel perfect collision calculations. These are used later for the platformer mini-game.

Chapter 9 Result

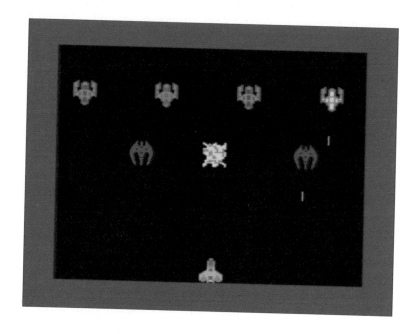

Chapter 10: Twinkle Twinkle Little Star

Open chapter10.cbmprj in CBM Prg Studio.

Custom Characters

As with the bullets, we create some custom characters to be used as background scrolling stars. These stars will scroll from the top to the bottom of the screen, therefore unlike the bullets we'll have a frame for each pixel movement vertically rather than horizontally.

Double click the characters.cst file in the Project Explorer to open the chapter 10 character file. The character numbers 72->79 have been reserved for the star animation frames.

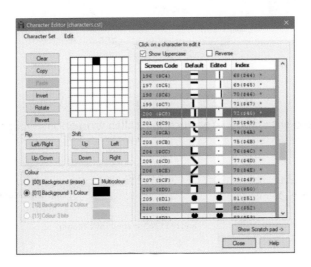

Save the character file with **Character Set->Save**, then export a binary version of the characters to be used in-game with **Character Set->Export->To Binary File**. Choose to export 80 characters starting at character 0 and name the file characters.bin in the project directory (Overwrite if necessary).

Star Movement

Star movement is performed by adding a subroutine call to update the stars code.

gameMain.asm

```
jsr gameStarsUpdate
```

There are 40 stars, one for each character column on the screen. Each star scrolls downwards. Every pixel movement selects a new animation frame. When the frame goes above 8, it wraps back around to the first frame and moves down a character on screen until it reaches the bottom of the screen, at which point it selects a new speed and color, then starts over.

The top row is left empty to accommodate the scores and lives later.

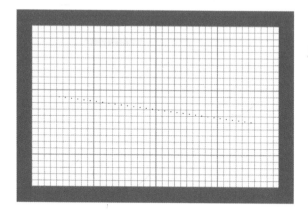

62

Two tables are used that contain a value for each of the 40 stars. starsYCharArray is the initial row Y start position, and starsSpeedColArray is the initial Color and Speed. Note the speed is equal to the color, i.e. each speed has its own color.

gameStars.asm

```
starsYCharArray   byte 15,  6, 17,  1, 18,  2,  4, 14, 12,  5
                  byte 13,  3,  9,  7, 10, 21,  5, 13, 10, 23
                  byte 11,  5, 15,  1,  5,  9,  7, 18, 11,  2
                  byte 12, 16, 21,  9,  2,  5, 16,  8, 15,  2


starsSpeedColArray byte 4,  2,  4,  3,  4,  3,  4,  3,  4,  3
                   byte 1,  2,  4,  2,  4,  2,  3,  4,  2,  3
                   byte 2,  3,  4,  3,  4,  1,  4,  3,  1,  3
                   byte 4,  3,  4,  1,  4,  2,  4,  2,  3,  2
```

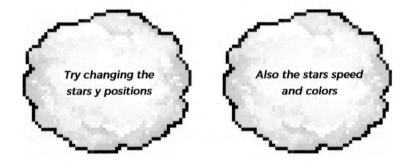

Try changing the stars y positions

Also the stars speed and colors

As a finishing touch, the border color is set to black to blend in with the starry background.

gameMain.asm

```
LIBSCREEN_SETCOLORS Black, Black, Black, Black, Black
```

Chapter 10 Result

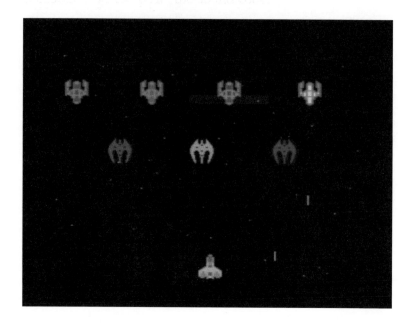

Chapter 11: Let There Be Sound

Open chapter11.cbmprj in CBM Prg Studio.

Execute Buffers

An execute buffer is a stream of information containing both commands and data. They're used extensively by graphics cards to send data to the GPU (Graphics Processing Unit).

The sound library has been implemented using an execute buffer to create a block of data describing the commands and data to send to the SID chip. This way our game can start a pre-created effect then continue processing. The sound library update code takes care of SID chip register changes over time.

Effects

Here's an example of a pre-created explosion sound effect. First is a NoiseEnd command to stop any sound that hasn't finished playing on this voice. Then the ADSR and frequency values are set and a NoiseStart command starts the SID chip actually playing the note. The delay command makes the update code do nothing but count down (holding the sustain volume) until 20 frames have passed, then a NoiseEnd command is sent to SID chip to stop the sound. At this point the Release happens before the sound ends. The high and low byte variables are an efficient way of passing the 16 bit location of this effect execute buffer to the play macro.

libSound.asm

```
soundExplosion    byte CmdWave, NoiseEnd
                  byte CmdAttackDecay, Attack_38ms+Decay_114ms
                  byte CmdSustainRelease,
Sustain_Vol10+Release_300ms
                  byte CmdFrequencyHigh, 21
                  byte CmdFrequencyLow, 31
                  byte CmdWave, NoiseStart
                  byte CmdDelay, 20
                  byte CmdWave, NoiseEnd
                  byte CmdEnd
soundExplosionHigh byte >soundExplosion
soundExplosionLow  byte <soundExplosion
```

Sound execute buffer processing is performed by adding a subroutine call to update the sound code.

gameMain.asm

```
jsr libSoundUpdate
```

Sounds are then played by triggering them at the appropriate point in the game code.

gamePlayer.asm

```
; play the firing sound
LIBSOUND_PLAY_VAA 0, soundFiringHigh, soundFiringLow

. . .

; play explosion sound
LIBSOUND_PLAY_VAA 1, soundExplosionHigh, soundExplosionLow
```

gameAliens.asm

```
; play explosion sound
LIBSOUND_PLAY_VAA 2, soundExplosionHigh, soundExplosionLow
```

Note they use different voices so that they can play at the same time.

Try creating and playing your own sound execute buffers

Chapter 12: Space Shooter Mini-Game

Open chapter12.cbmprj in CBM Prg Studio.

Game Flow

The final stage in creating our space shooter mini-game involves handling the game being in various states. i.e. in a menu, alive, or dying. Separating the game processing out like this allows various speed optimizations, as only the current state's code needs to be executed. E.g. We only need a check to start a new game if in the menu state.

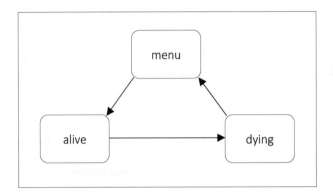

Subroutine calls are added to initialize and update the game flow.

gameMain.asm

```
jsr gameFlowInit

. . .

jsr gameFlowUpdate
```

The states are defined as constants and the current state is stored in the flowState variable.

gameFlow.asm

```
FlowStateMenu   = 0
FlowStateAlive  = 1
FlowStateDying  = 2

flowState byte FlowStateMenu
```

The processing of the game states is implemented using an efficient assembly language method called a jump table. The high and low address bytes of the state update subroutines are stored in a table.

gameFlow.asm

```
gameFlowJumpTableLow
        byte <gameFlowUpdateMenu
        byte <gameFlowUpdateAlive
        byte <gameFlowUpdateDying

gameFlowJumpTableHigh
        byte >gameFlowUpdateMenu
        byte >gameFlowUpdateAlive
        byte >gameFlowUpdateDying
```

Remember that
**< gets the low
byte and > gets
the high byte**

Then the game flow update subroutine selects between them based on the current game state.

```
gameFlowUpdate

        ; get the current state
        ldy flowState

        ; write the subroutine address to a zeropage location
        lda gameFlowJumpTableLow,y
        sta ZeroPageLow
        lda gameFlowJumpTableHigh,y
        sta ZeroPageHigh

        ; jump to the subroutine the zeropage location points to
        jmp (ZeroPageLow)
```

Some parts of the game call game flow subroutines as various events happen, such as to increase the score when an alien dies.

```
gameAliensUpdateCollisions

        . . .
        jsr gameFlowIncreaseScore
        . . .

        rts
```

And to decrease the number of lives when the player dies.

gamePlayer.asm

```
gamePlayerUpdateCollisions

        . . .
        jsr gameFlowPlayerDied
        . . .

        rts
```

The current game state can be changed to reflect the event e.g. switch from the Alive state to the Dying state.

gameFlow.asm

```
gameFlowPlayerDied

        . . .

        ; change state
        lda #FlowStateDying
        sta flowState

        rts
```

Scores and Lives

An efficient way to store and display the scores and lives is to use a decimal number representation. We have 6 digits for each of the scores with 2 digits per byte, and 2 digits for the lives covered with 1 byte.

```
                        gameFlow.asm
score1          byte 0
score2          byte 0
score3          byte 0

lives           byte 0

hiscore1        byte 0
hiscore2        byte 0
hiscore3        byte 0
```

The LIBSCREEN_DRAWTEXT_AAAV macro is called, passing in the character positions, a zero terminated string, and a text color.

```
                        gameFlow.asm
flowScoreText           text 'Score:'
                        byte 0

    . . .

LIBSCREEN_DRAWTEXT_AAAV flowScoreX, flowScoreY, flowScoreText,
White
```

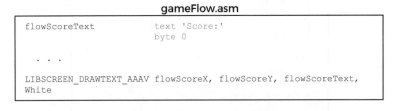

Try changing the string contents and color

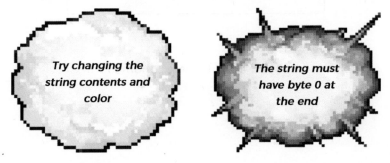

The string must have byte 0 at the end

The numbers are displayed by calling the decimal text drawing subroutine LIBSCREEN_DRAWDECIMAL_AAAV with a decimal number (representing 2 digits) and a text color. Each set of 2 digits is moved along 2 characters on the screen to line them up.

gameFlow.asm

```
gameFlowScoreDisplay

        LIBMATH_ADD8BIT_AVA flowScoreX, 6, flowScoreNumX
        LIBSCREEN_DRAWDECIMAL_AAAV flowScoreNumX, flowScoreY,
score3, White

        LIBMATH_ADD8BIT_AVA flowScoreX, 8, flowScoreNumX
        LIBSCREEN_DRAWDECIMAL_AAAV flowScoreNumX, flowScoreY,
score2, White

        LIBMATH_ADD8BIT_AVA flowScoreX, 10, flowScoreNumX
        LIBSCREEN_DRAWDECIMAL_AAAV flowScoreNumX, flowScoreY,
score1, White

        rts
```

As we don't draw to the top row of the screen, it's more efficient to only draw the scores and lives when they update, therefore these are called throughout the game flow code in the appropriate places.

The top row doesn't need to be drawn every frame

Memory Usage

The space shooter mini-game uses:

4582 bytes for code.

1024 bytes for 16 sprites.

640 bytes for 80 custom characters.

For a total of 6246 bytes or 6 Kilobytes.

The prg is 13K because the data is spread out leaving gaps in the memory map. This could be tightened up to reduce the prg size but having it setup like this leaves a lot of free code space for experimenting.

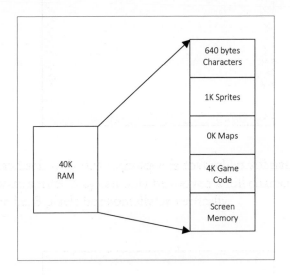

Now we have a complete space shooter mini-game. Enjoy!

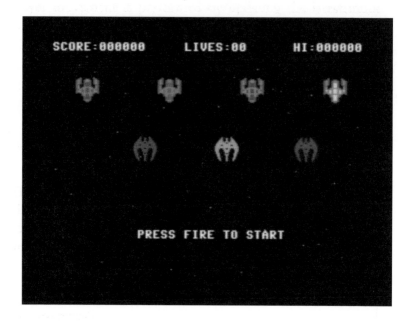

PART IV: LET'S MAKE A PLATFORMER

Chapter 13: Create a Cool Character

Open chapter13.cbmprj in CBM Prg Studio.

Player Animation

Double click the sprites.spt file in the Project Explorer to open the chapter 13 sprite file. Included are ten multicolor frames of character animation: 5 right facing, and 5 left facing. Preview the right facing walk animation by setting the Animation Start frame to 2, End frame to 4, then press Start. Slide the bar to change the animation speed.

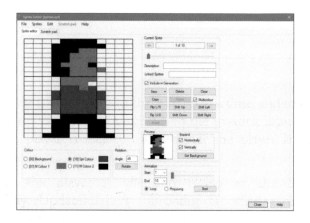

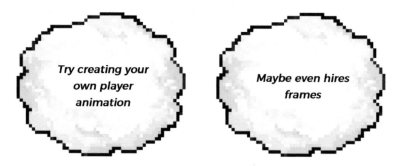

Try creating your own player animation

Maybe even hires frames

Save the sprite file with **File->Save**, then export a binary version of the sprites to be used in game with **File->Export->To Binary File**. Choose to save all the sprites and name the file sprites.bin in the project directory (Overwrite if necessary).

Player Movement

The movement code for the player is enhanced from Chapter 7 by storing the joystick input values into a velocity value in gamePlayerUpdateVelocity, then applying that to the position later in gamePlayerUpdatePosition.

There are two reasons for this. First, the velocity is stored as a signed value (see Chapter 1) so that the sign can be tested later to see which way the player is moving, and therefore which animation frames to use. Second, by storing a velocity we can gradually slow it down over time so when the player is jumping the movement is slowed down realistically, rather than stopping movement the moment the joystick is released.

gamePlayer.asm

```
gamePlayerUpdate

        jsr gamePlayerUpdateVelocity
        jsr gamePlayerUpdateState
        jsr gamePlayerUpdatePosition

        rts
```

The six separate animation states are implemented as a jump table similar to the state machine in Chapter 12, and are updated with the call to gamePlayerUpdateState.

gamePlayer.asm

```
; Jump Tables
gamePlayerJumpTableLow
        byte <gamePlayerUpdateIdleLeft
        byte <gamePlayerUpdateIdleRight
        byte <gamePlayerUpdateRunLeft
        byte <gamePlayerUpdateRunRight
        byte <gamePlayerUpdateJumpLeft
        byte <gamePlayerUpdateJumpRight

gamePlayerJumpTableHigh
        byte >gamePlayerUpdateIdleLeft
        byte >gamePlayerUpdateIdleRight
        byte >gamePlayerUpdateRunLeft
        byte >gamePlayerUpdateRunRight
        byte >gamePlayerUpdateJumpLeft
        byte >gamePlayerUpdateJumpRight
```

The player is only in one of these states at a time, and transition from state to state occurs based on the joystick input, which way the player is facing, and whether the player is on the ground.

E.g. If the player is idle and facing to the left, the gamePlayerUpdateIdleLeft subroutine is called each frame which calls the one of the state transition subroutines based on a negative or positive X velocity, and a playerOnGround variable.

gamePlayer.asm

```
gamePlayerUpdateIdleLeft

        lda playerXVelocity
        beq gPUILDone           ; if zero velocity

        bpl gPUILPositive
;gPUILNegative                   ; if negative velocity
        jsr gamePlayerSetRunLeft
        jmp gPUILDone
gPUILPositive                    ; if positive velocity
        jsr gamePlayerSetRunRight
gPUILDone

        ; Switch to jump state if not on ground
        lda playerOnGround
        bne gPUILNoJump
        jsr gamePlayerSetJumpLeft
gPUILNoJump

        rts
```

The state transition subroutines change the player animation state, stop any currently playing animation, and play the appropriate new animation.

gamePlayer.asm

```
gamePlayerSetIdleLeft

        lda #PlayerStateIdleLeft
        sta playerState
        LIBSPRITE_STOPANIM_A playerSprite
        LIBSPRITE_SETFRAME_AV playerSprite, PlayerIdleLeftAnim

        rts
```

Player Jumping

Friction is applied to the X velocity by reducing the velocity over time. However, it's only applied if the player is on the ground. Therefore if the player is off the ground i.e. jumping, the player continues horizontal movement even when the joystick is released.

gamePlayer.asm

```
; x velocity -----------------------------------------------
        lda playerOnGround ; apply friction if on ground
        beq gPUVNoFriction
        lda #0
        sta playerXVelocity
gPUVNoFriction
        . . .
```

When the jump button is pressed, a boost is applied to the Y velocity in the up direction. Gravity is applied each frame which slows down the up movement, and as a signed number is used for the Y velocity this eventually turns into down movement until the player reaches PlayerYMax (screen Y goes from 0 at the top and increases downwards) at which point the Y position is clamped to the ground.

gamePlayer.asm

```
    . . .

; y velocity -----------------------------------------------

        ; apply gravity
        inc playerYVelocity

        ; apply jump velocity if on ground & jump pressed
        lda playerOnGround
        beq gPUVNojump
        LIBINPUT_GETFIREPRESSED
        bne gPUVNoJump
        LIBMATH_SUB8BIT_AVA playerYVelocity, PlayerJumpAmount,
playerYVelocity
        lda #False
        sta playerOnGround
gPUVNoJump

        . . .
```

In addition to the standard jump movement, a 'Mario style' jump feature has been implemented. If the jump button is not held down while jumping then the y velocity boost applied is clamped to a lower value than usual. This has the effect of increasing the jump height if you do hold down the jump button.

Button released after jump

Button held after jump

Try changing
PlayerJumpAmount
for max height
adjustment

Try changing
PlayerYVelocityMax
for small jump
adjustment

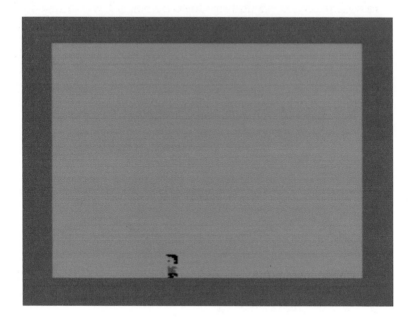

Chapter 14: Add a Scrolling Background

Open chapter14.cbmprj in CBM Prg Studio.

Custom Characters

Double click the characters.cst file to open some pre-created custom characters. Click **Show Scratch pad** to open a temporary work space to test characters placed together.

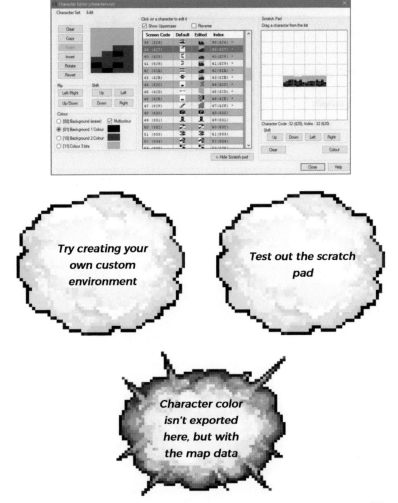

Try creating your own custom environment

Test out the scratch pad

Character color isn't exported here, but with the map data

Save the character file with **Character Set->Save**, then export a binary version of the characters to be used in game with **Character Set->Export->To Binary File**. Choose to export 100 characters starting at character 0 and name the file characters.bin in the project directory (Overwrite if necessary).

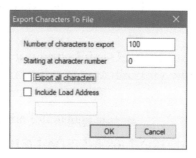

Screen Map Data

Double click the screens.sdd file to open six pre-created level screens. Move through the screens by clicking the arrows in the **Navigation** section. The screens look garbled because they're using the standard C64 character set and not our custom characters.

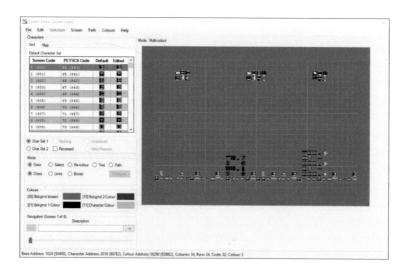

Load the previously saved custom character set into the Screen Editor with **File->Load character set**.

The two bottom rows are left empty to accommodate the scores and time later.

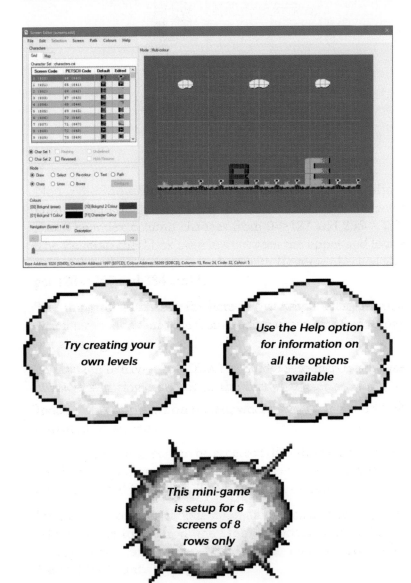

Try creating your own levels

Use the Help option for information on all the options available

This mini-game is setup for 6 screens of 8 rows only

A maximum of 8 rows per frame can be scrolled using the code presented here to maintain 60 frames per second. This has been segregated into 2 rows for the clouds and 6 rows for the environment. Therefore all other rows must remain empty. (It is possible to scroll an entire screen each frame using more advanced techniques – see Chapter 20).

Export the map data using **File->Export Assembler** to a file called screens.bin in the project directory with the following options (Overwrite if necessary).

Generate using the following list:

1-6(3),1-6(4),1-6(18),1-6(19),1-6(20),1-6(21),1-6(22),1-6(23)

(This specifies screens 1-6 row 3, row 4, row 18 etc.)

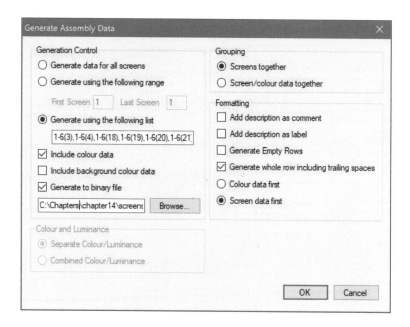

Map Setup

The exported map data is added to the program by including it in the memory map. The *= $1F20 directive tells the assembler to start placing data at memory location $1F20 onwards (See Chapter 2 – Memory for our chosen data placement scheme).

gameMemory.asm

```
* = $1F20
        incbin screens.bin
```

In the game initialize code, the screen is set to multicolor and a subroutine is called to initialize the map data.

gameMain.asm

```
        LIBSCREEN_SETMULTICOLORMODE
        . . .
        jsr gameMapInit
```

Each of the map rows previously saved is copied to the appropriate row on the screen (Note the rows are 0 based in code but start from 1 in the screen export settings). E.g.

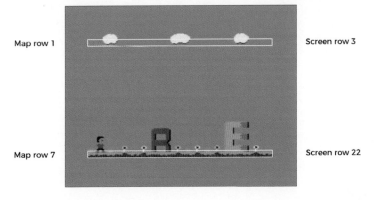

Map row 1 — Screen row 3

Map row 7 — Screen row 22

Map Scrolling

The C64 has hardware registers that assist in scrolling the screen horizontally or vertically. They can be set between 0 and 7 in the X and Y directions to shift the screen display by that many pixels.

To scroll the screen we wait until the player reaches a threshold line, then begin adjusting the hardware X scroll register a pixel at a time until it reaches the maximum offset. At that point, the whole screen's map data is shifted across by a column and re-copied to the screen, then the hardware register is reset. Repeating this process has the result of a smooth scroll in the required direction.

The C64 also has a mode to set the number of columns displayed to 38 rather than 40. This is so that it's not noticeable as a new column is updated onto the edges of the screen. The data is still copied there but it's hidden from view. We set this in the game initialize code.

gameMain.asm

```
LIBSCREEN_SET38COLUMNMODE
```

The gameMapUpdate subroutine updates the map data to the screen when required using the screenColumn variable as an offset into the map data. The screenColumn variable is incremented or decremented as the player moves past the set screen thresholds and the hardware scroll register has wrapped around 0->7.

GameMap.asm

```
gameMapUpdate

        ; no need to update the cloud colors or map row 7 colors
        ; as they have the same colors across the row

        ; clouds characters
        LIBSCREEN_COPYMAPROW_VVA 0, 2, screenColumn
        LIBSCREEN_COPYMAPROW_VVA 1, 3, screenColumn

        ; ground characters
        LIBSCREEN_COPYMAPROW_VVA 2, 17, screenColumn
        LIBSCREEN_COPYMAPROW_VVA 3, 18, screenColumn
        LIBSCREEN_COPYMAPROW_VVA 4, 19, screenColumn
        LIBSCREEN_COPYMAPROW_VVA 5, 20, screenColumn
        LIBSCREEN_COPYMAPROW_VVA 6, 21, screenColumn
        LIBSCREEN_COPYMAPROW_VVA 7, 22, screenColumn

        ; ground colors
        LIBSCREEN_COPYMAPROWCOLOR_VVA 2, 17, screenColumn
        LIBSCREEN_COPYMAPROWCOLOR_VVA 3, 18, screenColumn
        LIBSCREEN_COPYMAPROWCOLOR_VVA 4, 19, screenColumn
        LIBSCREEN_COPYMAPROWCOLOR_VVA 5, 20, screenColumn
        LIBSCREEN_COPYMAPROWCOLOR_VVA 6, 21, screenColumn

        rts
```

The gamePlayerClampXandScroll subroutine is called from the gamePlayerUpdate position subroutine and handles when to call gameMapUpdate based on the X and Y player threshold values.

gamePlayer.asm

```
jsr gamePlayerClampXandScroll
```

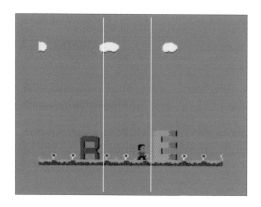

Try adjusting the min/max scroll thresholds

Collisions

The LIBSCREEN_PIXELTOCHAR_AAVAVAAAA macro
is used to calculate the player's character position. We expand
on the previous mini-game by making use of the pixel offsets
calculated to perform pixel accurate collision detection.

We start by defining 4 collision points relative to the top-left
corner of the player sprite.

gamePlayer.asm

```
PlayerLeftCollX          = 4
PlayerLeftCollY          = 14
PlayerRightCollX         = 20
PlayerRightCollY         = 14
PlayerBottomLeftCollX    = 7
PlayerBottomLeftCollY    = 20
PlayerBottomRightCollX   = 13
PlayerBottomRightCollY   = 20
```

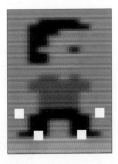

The player code now calls a subroutine to update the collisions
with the background.

gamePlayer.asm

```
gamePlayerUpdate

        . . .
        jsr gamePlayerUpdateBackgroundCollisions
        . . .

        rts
```

The gameUpdateBackgroundCollisions subroutine transforms each of the collision points into world space by adding the sprite's position, then calls a collision response subroutine (which will adjust the position if a collision occurred), then transforms the point back to sprite space and applies it to the player's position.

gamePlayer.asm

```
        . . .

; Transform right collision point
        LIBMATH_ADD16BIT_AAVVAA playerXHigh, playerXLow, 0,
PlayerRightCollX, playerCollXHigh, playerCollXLow
        LIBMATH_ADD8BIT_AVA playerY, PlayerRightCollY,
playerCollY

        ; Run collision check & response
        jsr gamePlayerCollideRight

        ; Transform back to sprite space
        LIBMATH_SUB16BIT_AAVVAA playerCollXHigh, playerCollXLow,
0, PlayerRightCollX, playerXHigh, playerXLow
        LIBMATH_SUB8BIT_AVA playerCollY, PlayerRightCollY,
playerY

        . . . ,
```

The collision response subroutines check if the current background character should be collided with and if so, align the position on an 8 pixel boundary. This is a very fast method of collision response and relies on the fact that all of our background characters are aligned.

gamePlayer.asm

```
gamePlayerCollideRight

        ; Find the screen character at the player position
        LIBSCREEN_PIXELTOCHAR_AAVAVAAAA playerCollXHigh,
playerCollXLow, 24, playerCollY, 50, playerXChar, playerXOffset,
playerYChar, playerYOffset
        LIBSCREEN_SETCHARPOSITION_AA playerXChar, playerYChar
        LIBSCREEN_GETCHAR ZeroPageTemp

        ; Handle any collisions with character code > 32
        lda #32
        cmp ZeroPageTemp
        bcs gPCRNoCollision

        ; Collision response
        lda playerCollXLow
        and #%11111000
        sta playerCollXLow
gPCRNoCollision

        rts
```

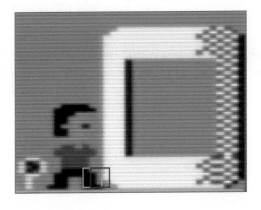

Chapter 14 Result

Chapter 15: Pick Up the Pickups

Open chapter15.cbmprj in CBM Prg Studio.

Collection

In each of the three player collision subroutines (and therefore once for each player collision point) a call is made to the gamePickupsHandle subroutine.

gamePlayer.asm

```
gamePlayerCollideRight

    . . .
    ; Handle any pickups (char 0)
    jsr gamePickupsHandle
    . . .

    rts
```

This subroutine checks if the screen character that the collision point is touching is character number 0. We've arbitrarily assigned character 0 to be the pickup character and drawn it as a flower in the custom character set.

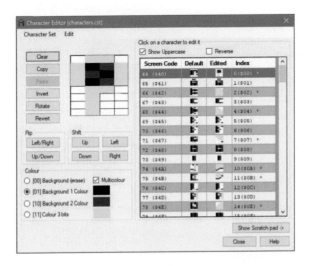

If the player collides with a pickup, a space character is set at that position on screen to make it disappear, and also a space character is set at the current location in the map data. If this wasn't done then the pickup would reappear when the screen scrolls and the map data is refreshed to the screen.

The pickup information is then stored in a list to provide the ability to reset later.

gamePickups.asm

```
gamePickupsHandle

        lda ZeroPageTemp
        bne gPHNoPickup ; is the character a 0? i.e. a pickup

        ; clear the screen position
        LIBSCREEN_SETCHAR_V SpaceCharacter

        ; clear the map position
        LIBSCREEN_SETMAPCHAR_VAAV PickupMapRow, screenColumn,
playerXChar, SpaceCharacter

        ; add the map position to the reset list
        ldx pickupsNumResetItems
        lda screenColumn
        sta pickupsColumnArray,X
        lda playerXChar
        sta pickupsXCharArray,X
        inc pickupsNumResetItems
gPHNoPickup

        rts
```

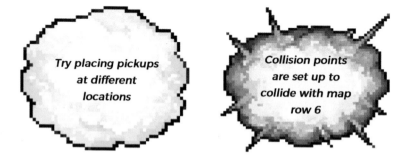

Try placing pickups at different locations

Collision points are set up to collide with map row 6

Reset

The reset subroutine will be called later in Chapter 17 when we reach the end of game and the pickups need to be repositioned. The subroutine loops through all previously stored pickups, places a 0 back into the correct map data location, then empties the list.

gamePickups.asm

```
gamePickupsReset

        lda pickupsNumResetItems
        beq gPRDone

        ldx #0
gPRLoop
        ; reset the map position to a pickup char 0
        lda pickupsColumnArray,X
        sta pickupsColumn
        lda pickupsXCharArray,X
        sta pickupsXChar
        LIBSCREEN_SETMAPCHAR_VAAV PickupMapRow, pickupsColumn,
pickupsXChar, 0

        inx
        cpx pickupsNumResetItems
        bmi gPRLoop

        lda #0
        sta pickupsNumResetItems
gPRDone

        rts
```

Chapter 16: Dig Up Those Pesky Worms

Open chapter16.cbmprj in CBM Prg Studio.

Enemy Animation

Double click the sprites.spt file in the Project Explorer to open the chapter 16 sprite file. Included are six multicolor frames of a worm enemy animation: 3 right facing, and 3 left facing. Preview the right facing animation by setting the Animation Start frame to 11, End frame to 13, then press Start. Slide the bar to change the animation speed.

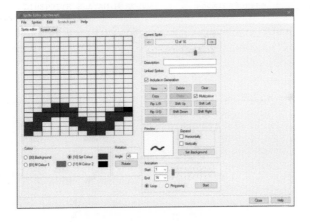

The enemies are placed by the character X value in a table, along with how far they should move.

```
                            gameEnemies.asm
enemiesXCharArray        byte    21,  37,   55,   79, 113, 151, 189

  . . .

enemiesXMoveArray        byte    63,  95,  136,  136, 160, 112, 151

  . . .
```

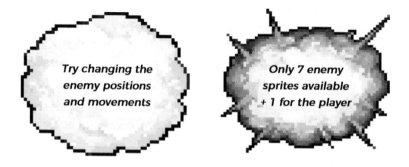

Try changing the enemy positions and movements

Only 7 enemy sprites available + 1 for the player

In the game initialize code, a subroutine is called to initialize the enemies.

```
                            gameMain.asm
        jsr gameEnemiesInit
```

As with the player, the enemies are initialized by enabling the sprite, setting the current animation frame and setting the sprite colors. However this time the code loops around for each of the 7 enemies (EnemiesMax=7).

As an extra graphical touch, the player and enemy sprites have their priority set to background with the macro LIBSPRITE_SETPRIORITY_AV so they draw behind the grass and flowers.

gameEnemies.asm

```
gameEnemiesInit

        ldx #0
        stx enemiesSprite
gEILoop
        inc enemiesSprite ; x+1

        LIBSPRITE_SETFRAME_AV            enemiesSprite, 11
        LIBSPRITE_SETCOLOR_AV           enemiesSprite, Brown
        LIBSPRITE_MULTICOLORENABLE_AV   enemiesSprite, True
        LIBSPRITE_SETPRIORITY_AV        enemiesSprite, True
        LIBSPRITE_PLAYANIM_AVVVV        enemiesSprite, 10, 12,
EnemyAnimDelay, True

        ; loop for each enemy
        inx
        cpx #EnemiesMax
        bne gEILoop

        rts
```

Try changing the enemy sprite values

Enemy Movement

In the game update code, a subroutine is called to update the enemies.

gameMain.asm

```
jsr gameEnemiesUpdate
```

The on-screen character X position is calculated by adding the start character position from the XChar Array to the screenColumn variable that's tracked when the screen scrolls. If this falls between 0 and 39 then the enemy's movement is updated.

The movement is updated by adding the enemiesXOffset variable which moves backwards and forwards between 0 and the value in the XMove Array.

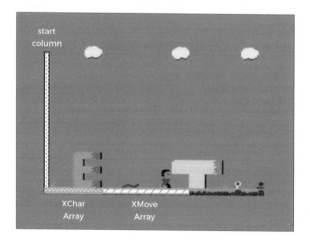

Chapter 17: Platformer Mini-Game

Open chapter17.cbmprj in CBM Prg Studio.

The platformer mini-game is setup similar to the space shooter mini-game with a few small additions.

Timer

To replace a lives display we have a timer. A subroutine is called every frame from the alive state to count down.

gameFlow.asm

```
gameFlowUpdateAlive

        jsr gameFlowDecreaseTime ; countdown time

        rts
```

To stop the score line from scrolling, the hardware X scroll register is set to 0 at scanline 235, then reset to the correct value at the end of gamePlayerUpdate.

gameMain.asm

```
        LIBSCREEN_WAIT_V 235 ; Wait for scanline 235

        ; reset the scroll register for the score line
        LIBSCREEN_SETSCROLLXVALUE_V 0
```

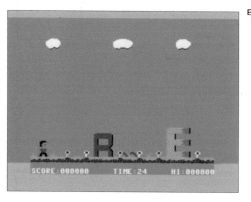

End player
update

Scanline
235

Death

There are three ways to die.

If the time reaches 0 in the gameFlowDecreaseTime subroutine, then the gameFlowPlayerDied subroutine is called.

In each of the three player collision subroutines (and therefore once for each player collision point) a call is made to the gamePlayerDeathCharsHandle subroutine. This calls the gameFlowPlayerDied subroutine if there's been a collision with character number 60 or 61 (the spikes).

gamePlayer.asm

```
gamePlayerCollideRight
        . . .
        jsr gamePlayerDeathCharsHandle
        . . .
        rts
```

The player update code now calls a subroutine to check the hardware collision register for a sprite to sprite collision. As we don't need to know which sprite collided, it's a good use for this method of collision detection.

gamePlayer.asm

```
gamePlayerUpdate
        . . .
        jsr gamePlayerUpdateSpriteCollisions
        . . .
        rts

. . .

gamePlayerUpdateSpriteCollisions

        LIBSPRITE_DIDCOLLIDEWITHSPRITE_A playerSprite
        beq gPUSCNoCollide
        jsr gameFlowPlayerDied

gPUSCNoCollide
        rts
```

Memory Usage

The platformer mini-game uses:

5499 bytes for code.

3840 bytes for 6 map screens.

1792 bytes for 28 sprites.

800 bytes for 100 custom characters.

For a total of 11931 bytes or 12 Kilobytes approx.

This prg of 13K is much closer to the data size used as much more of the empty space has been utilized. Remember there is still 28K of RAM free in the block that we are using (without swapping out the KERNAL ROM or BASIC).

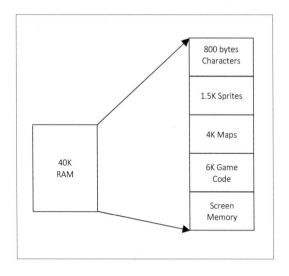

Now we have a complete platformer mini-game. Enjoy!

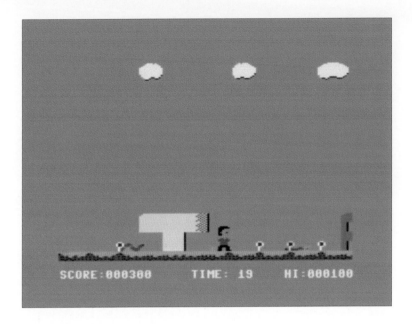

PART V: RUNNING ON THE HARDWARE

Chapter 18: What Do I Need?

If you prefer an authentic retro gaming experience, here's a selection of equipment to run your games on.

Most of the original hardware can be sourced from online auction sites, but remember that some items listed here are over 30 years old, therefore parts can fail. However, it's fairly simple with salvaged spares and a little soldering experience to return these machines back to their former glory.

Computer

The original Commodore 64 known as the breadbin.

The Commodore 64C. Essentially a C64 with a facelift.

The Commodore 128. More powerful with extra memory. Also has a C64 mode.

The C64 Mini. This new hardware is due to be released soon and emulates a C64. It could be a viable alternative if it supports running your own program files.

https://thec64.com/

Display

The Commodore 1701/2 Monitor. For the most authentic experience, a CRT monitor is recommended. However, CRT TV's or more modern monitors can be used providing they have a composite video input.

Joystick

The 9 pin Atari compatible style joystick. The excellent Competition Pro is pictured but there are many other types available.

Storage

The original Commodore 64 used tapes or 5.25" floppy disks for storage. There are now more efficient ways of transferring our program files to the hardware.

The SD2IEC emulates the workings of a Commodore 1541 disk drive using an SD card for storage. An excellent budget option but doesn't work with some games that require more precise 1541 features. (It does work with all of the prg's in this book). https://www.thefuturewas8bit.com/

The Ultimate II+ implements the precise functionality of a 1541 drive in hardware using a USB drive for storage. Compatible with almost every game, but comes at a higher price. http://1541ultimate.net

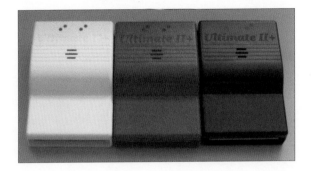

Fast Loader

These cartridges plug into the cartridge port of the Commodore 64/128 and accelerate loading speeds by many times. Games load in seconds rather than minutes.

The original Epyx Fast Load cartridge.

The Epyx Fastload RELOADED. A modern day equivalent.
https://www.thefuturewas8bit.com/

Chapter 19: Look, it's On My TV

To run your own prg files on the Commodore hardware:

- Build the prg file in CBM prg Studio.
- Copy the prg file to a memory card or USB stick (depending on the storage device used).
- Open the storage device file browser and navigate to and select the prg file.

That's it. There's not much to it!

Here's some links covering the specific storage device usage:

SD2IEC

https://www.thefuturewas8bit.com/index.php/sd2iec-info

https://www.thegeekpub.com/9473/sd2iec-manual-use-sd2iec-c64/

Ultimate II

http://1541ultimate.net/content/index.php

https://youtu.be/F6m6_Kb9c9U

PART VI: FURTHER LEARNING

Chapter 20: Advanced Topics

There are many more advanced features that the Commodore 64 can perform. These require expert understanding of the hardware, but the time taken to learn can produce a game of a professional standard.

Interrupts – The 6510 microprocessor can accept a signal that causes it to halt execution, run a custom subroutine, then return to where it was previously. This allows for precise timing to run code. E.g. to control graphical timings, when an effect has to occur at an exact position on the screen.

Full Screen Scrolling - It's possible to scroll the entire screen at 60fps using a combination of interrupt timing and double screen buffering techniques.

Sprite Multiplexing – The VIC-II has support for 8 hardware sprites. Technically, 8 sprites can be drawn on any scanline. Therefore, by updating the sprite registers at various scanlines (using interrupts), the sprites can be changed many times per screen refresh allowing more to be drawn on screen.

Music Player – Using precise interrupt timing, music player code can process lists of music data and play full songs independent of the main game code.

Extended Color Mode (ECM) – A screen mode that acts like multicolor mode and also allows a different background color per character, but has a more complex color encoding method and limits the number of unique characters to 64.

Loading/Saving – Transferring game data to disk or tape.

TV Standard – NTSC at 60 fps with 263 raster lines vs PAL at 50 fps with 312 raster lines. These differences can be addressed by scaling the game update timings and rearranging the display.

If this book was useful and you'd like to see additional content covering these advanced techniques and more, let me know on the forum at www.retrogamedev.com.

Chapter 21: Useful Resources and Wrap Up

Books:
Commodore 64 Programmers Reference Guide
Mapping the Commodore 64 – Sheldon Leemon
Assembly Language Programming with the Commodore 64 –
Marvin L. De Jong

Community:
http://codebase64.org/
http://www.lemon64.com/forum/

Publishers:
http://pondsoft.uk/
https://www.protovision.games/
http://www.psytronik.net/newsite/
http://www.rgcd.co.uk/

Tools:
CBM Prg Studio - http://www.ajordison.co.uk/
VICE Emulator - http://vice-emu.sourceforge.net/

To create a complete game to the required standard for one of the publishers above can take in excess of year, and many, many hours of learning and hard work. I hope this book provides inspiration to start you on that journey.

Let's strive to create a whole new wave of published games for the retro systems to keep them alive. After all, without them and the people who created them, there'd be no games industry!

Acknowledgements

Thanks to the following for their knowledgeable feedback:

Jay Aldred – Creator of Galencia C64

http://www.galencia.games

Graham Axten – Creator of Bear Essentials C64

http://pondsoft.uk/bear.html

For the extensive feedback and tool support:

Arthur Jordison – Creator of CBM Prg Studio

http://www.ajordison.co.uk/

For the amazing cover design and artistic input:

Rick Nath and Andy Jackson

http://surface3d.co.uk

Index

Printed in Great Britain
by Amazon